THE BETRAYAL

By

JOYCE LOMAS CUSHENBERRY

Empoword Publishing Worldwide

17127 Wax Rd Ste A

Greenwell Springs, LA 70739

www.EmpowordPublishing.com

(225) 412-3130

Kingdom are vested in the Crown. Reproduced by permission of the Crown's patentee, Cambridge University Press.

Paperback ISBN: 979-8-324-55446-0

TABLE OF CONTENTS

"What therefore God hath joined together, let not man put asunder"

–Mark 10:9 (KJV)

DEDICATION

This book is dedicated in remembrance of my dad Henry, and my mom Rosa. I would also like to dedicate this book to my sister Myra, who encouraged me to stay strong. My brother Malcolm, stepped up to the plate when needed.

CHAPTER 1:
HIGH SCHOOL STUDENTS

I had been seeing Al for about a year, nothing serious; we were just high school students. My father was very strict and besides, I had already ended the relationship. No one was able to come to my house on a school night, so Al was only able to come to my house on Saturdays, when it started getting close to 10:00 p.m., my dad started clearing his throat and the boys knew it was time to go.

So, when Al left my house, I heard he went to Janell's house. I guess her dad approved of a guy coming to his house after 10:00 p.m. or maybe he wasn't aware of somebody coming to his house to see his daughter. We were all high school students. The next thing I heard, was that Janell was pregnant. Pregnancy required in those days you had to get married. It was called a shotgun wedding. Nine months later, the baby was here. Whenever Janell was gone, Al would call me. I would talk to him, but was not interested in a relationship with him. I had already ended the relationship when I found out he was going to her house often after 10:00 P.M. What made him think I was interested? Apparently, he wasn't happy, life wasn't what he had expected. I stopped taking Al's calls because he had told a family member that we were going to get back together.

Al started seeing a girl and making more babies. He didn't stay with his first child's mom.

I never believed in shotgun weddings. I want to get married without being forced. I never wanted, a guy to marry me just to give the baby his name.

Whenever I went out with friends, I had to get home by 10:00 p.m. I respect my parents and appreciate my upbringing. My parents believed that after ten you would end up in the bed with a guy. I knew my dad didn't "play" so, I made sure not to get into trouble.

CHAPTER 2:
THE BASKETBALL GAME

I remember sitting in the gym on this cool November night watching the basketball game. The Broncos were leading 10-6, it was a good game. Basketball has always been my favorite sport. A group of friends and I, always make plans to go to the games. Most of the time four of us would work the concession stands. This tall handsome guy caught my attention as he walked out of the lobby into the gym. He was dressed in jeans, a nice plaid long-sleeved shirt, and Timberland shoes. I just had to meet him, so I asked a friend who knew him to introduce me to him. The game was approximately 3 minutes and 22 seconds left. Broncos led 113; The Panthers had 96. After the game, she introduced me to him and I was impressed. I liked what I saw.

CHAPTER 3:
THE SURPRISE VISIT

L ater that week, I got a visit from him. I didn't give him my address, but he had gotten my cousin to bring him to my house. We started dating. Eight months later, he went to California to stay with his grandfather and search for a job. He wanted to secure our relationship, so he gave me an engagement ring before leaving and I accepted. I had graduated high school and was pursuing a nursing career.

CHAPTER 4:
A CORRESPONDED
RELATIONSHIP

W e corresponded by mail and every Sunday, he called me on a pay phone. He would talk for a long time; I would hear the operator asking him to add more coins for more minutes to talk. Sundays, I would get my call between 5:00 p.m. and 7:00 p.m. I took lots of pictures wearing different outfits and mailed them to him. He would write back and call on Sunday to let me know he had gotten the pictures and liked them.

CHAPTER 5:

DISTURBING NEWS

A s he reached his second year in San Francisco, I learned he was dating while I was being faithful. That upset me. Then, I found out that a girl had gotten pregnant for him in San Francisco. I mailed him his engagement ring back. I called my cousin Stacey in New Orleans; I told her I had just broken my engagement. I asked her whether I could come for the weekend to celebrate and she said yes. Stacey loved to party. I went down that Friday. She called her guy friend, who invited two more of his friends. Stacy, Claudia, and I met them at 9:00 p.m. at a club called "The Spot". Stacey brought Claudia and I. Jewel is Stacy's friend. He brought along two older guys. I could live with that. It was only for one night. Everybody was having fun. There were Go-Go dancers at the club. The later it got, the more people were coming in. Jewel paired Claudia with Earl. They paired me with Mitch. Like I said, an older guy. He was approximately 5' 11'' tall, on the slim side, dressed well, wearing a hat and Stacey Adam shoes. Mitch seemed to be a cool guy. We all danced and got to know each other. I found out Earl's relatives were from the same town I was from.

We left that club and went to another club called the "Walk Easy." We hung out there. There was so much smoke in the "Walk Easy" that I had to put my shades on. My eyes were steadily making tears. We left the "Walk Easy" and headed to a restaurant over on Orleans Avenue, "The Anderson." I ordered a medium rare steak with a baked potato, green salad, and toast. That was the best steak I had ever ordered. We got home at 7:00 a.m. Stacy, Claudia, and I planned to sleep all day and get ready for another night.

I enjoyed myself in New Orleans that weekend. I deserved that after all my efforts in a relationship that didn't work out. Sometimes it just pays to get out and have fun. It seemed like Dave was enjoying himself.

CHAPTER 6:
WHAT'S COMING NEXT?

———————•———————

Two weeks later, Dave arrived at my door trying to explain. I was surprised, I didn't expect to see Dave at my door. I had ended the engagement. I had sent him his engagement ring back. For some unknown reason, I forgave him. We got back together and he proposed to me. I accepted on December 13, we were married that year. My dad and my uncle didn't want me to marry him. My dad knew his dad and my dad said, "A young colt will saddle the same way a stallion will."

My uncle wanted to talk to me so I sat down at the table with him. He wanted to know whether I was sure I wanted to get married. My uncle felt I was too young and that I should enjoy myself before doing so.

Dave loved his grandfather Al a lot. Al had retired and would play cards with his friends, about every day of the week. Dave would brag about how Al's could make a great gumbo. Dave said, "Al found out I had sent him his engagement ring back". Al told him "That's the girl for you; Dave you better go get her". So, he took his grandfather's advice and left California to go get his fiancée back.

I don't think Mrs. Reed, Dave's mom wanted him to get married. Dave was Mrs. Reed's financial supporter. She bought cars and he helped her pay for them. Whenever Dave had somewhere to go, she would let him use the car except for one instance when Mrs. Reed let his brother Brad use the car. Dave was very upset about that because he felt he was paying the car notes and, Brad only cared about Brad. He never helped anybody with anything. Brad was a money borrower, who never paid back.

I remember once when Dave was upset because Brad needed a co-signer for a set of tires for his car. Dave co-signed for him. Brad paid one payment on that set of tires. Dave got stuck with the bill.

Dave also had a younger brother and sister who looked up to him. On pay day he would give them an allowance.

CHAPTER 7:
THE WEDDING

———————◆———————

My grandmother's wish was for me to find a good husband.

My wedding consisted of one maid of honor, one matron of honor, and four bridesmaids. I chose a beautiful pink; the dresses were long and they all held white mums. I gave all the bridesmaids jewelry as a gift for being in the wedding. The grooms wore black tuxes and black shoes. The flower girl was so cute and our ring bearer was perfect. The wedding was beautiful. The minister, Reverend Jones seemed to be a little nervous. Deep in my heart, when I was repeating my vows I meant all except for the worst. I meant I would stay with my husband in sickness, but not worse. I would do my best, but I wouldn't stay for the worst because I was going to make my life miserable or make myself sick from stress.

Lots of people attended my wedding invited and uninvited. Everyone seemed like they had a good time.

My mom Annie and her cousin Clara had prepared all kinds of food for our wedding reception. The food was good. Lots to drink. The cake was beautiful. Everybody complimented my mom.

CHAPTER 8:

THE HONEYMOON IS OVER

I was the oldest of three children. My sister Lynn and my brother Mel. There was a big age difference I was eleven years older than Lynn and fifteen years older than Mel.

We honeymooned in New Orleans. I was so in love we spent a week in New Orleans. The journey began. I am Mrs. Dave Lee.

We rented a small house not far from my parents. Lots of times I would bring my food and pots to my mom's house, so she could help me prepare a meal for Dave. I wanted to do home-cooked meals instead of frozen meals from the freezer heated up in the oven. That gets old after a period. Eventually, I learned to cook. I must say I became a darned good cook. Dave would stop at roadside stands to buy fruits and vegetables. He was a picky eater.

I was a very clean person, but I caught Dave looking under the bed, passing his finger on the floor to see if I had cleaned under the bed. He never knew I saw him my floors were so clean, you could eat off it. Just like the old saying.

On Saturdays, Dave always washed my car and his truck. I would work in the flower beds. If I needed help with the flower beds, Dave would help.

I was happy or so I thought. The ink on the marriage license hadn't dried. He was seeing someone else. I found out that Dave was seeing the cleaning lady at the place where we went to pick up our marriage license. I could see the lady was embarrassed, but I didn't know why.

CHAPTER 9:

TRAUMATIZED

I was so traumatized by all the unfaithfulness, that I lost my appetite and couldn't eat. I wore a size 7-9. I lost so much weight my clothes were just hanging on me. I told myself I had to start eating. Dave wasn't losing weight, he was gaining. I wanted so much for the marriage to work, but that meant both of us. I am giving 100% and Dave wasn't even giving 50%. Dave often says, "You can't fight fire with fire you must fight fire with water". He had a lot of sayings and they all were for his benefit.

Going to work helped me to forget my problems. When I was at work, I focused on my patients. I liked taking care of people which is why I became a nurse.

When I was in high school, my dad's, mom became ill. Granny

was in and out of the hospital. My dad's sisters took turns sitting with her. When it was time for my dad to sit, I would always go in his place.

CHAPTER 10:

LOOKING BACK BEFORE AND AFTER THE MARRIAGE

B efore I married into Dave's family, he would bring me to his house on Sundays. The house was in the country; the only stores out there were convenience stores. If you forgot something that you didn't want to purchase at the convenience store you would have to drive twenty-five miles to the city.

Dave loved his father. Dave would talk about him a lot. He said everywhere he went; his father would bring him. Dave's father died when he was nine years old. Dave said his father started having seizures after getting hit on the head with a ball while playing baseball.

Dave wanted to go out with the guys. I didn't want him to go. I felt like it was girls, not the guys. When he was getting ready to walk out the door, I grabbed both back pockets of his pants. He was pulling one way and I was pulling the other way; his pants pocket came off the pants. You know Dave was furious. He put on another pair of pants and left anyway. I was upset he left anyway. He got back home after 12:00 a.m.

The next weekend was Easter Sunday. I had gotten ready for church and my dress was beautiful. Just as I was about to leave, Dave grabbed the shoulders of my dress and tore it off of me. I was stunned. He said that's for tearing my pant pockets off. Later when I regrouped, I had to laugh. I didn't let Dave see me laughing. I didn't make it to church because my dress was torn.

I had to make better plans than tearing clothes off each other. Another weekend came and Dave got ready to go out. I was prepared and ready. When he got into the truck, I got in too. Dave asked, "Where are you going"? I said, "With you." For some Godly reason, he had a change of plans, Dave no longer wanted to go out. He got out of his truck went back into the house and watched television the rest of the night.

Later that week, Dave left early one morning and returned later that evening around 4:30 p.m. with the window on the driver's side broken out. Dave's explanation was he was passing a large truck on the road; something flew off the truck and hit his window on the driver's side. The window on the driver's side was broken out. Later that week, I heard that one of his lady friends broke the window out because she was mad at him. She heard he was seeing someone else.

His sister Sue was a tall slender girl with long black hair and big brown eyes and her husband Kenny, who is Dave's brother-in-law, lived with Mrs. Reed. Dave's mom and grandmother were good cooks. His grandmother had retired from the school system. Dave's mom was still working in the school system. I enjoyed the food every Sunday. They would make smothered chicken, rice, potato salad, green beans, cinnamon rolls, and popcorn balls with pecans, and on some Sundays, they would make vanilla ice cream. They would pull out the hand crank ice cream maker and the men would take turns churning the ice cream until it was the right consistency. I picked up a lot of good pointers on cooking. I enjoyed watching everyone eat sweets. While growing up, my Easter basket would have candy in it from one Easter to the next Easter.

Dave's brother-in-law would fight Dave's sister Sue just about every weekend. That made Dave furious and his brother Brad. Kenny was an ex-marine who was well-built and had just gotten out of the service. That was why they were staying with Dave's mom.

I never knew what the fight was about. Sue was a sweet girl. I just assumed he had anger issues. After the fight, he would take the six-month-old baby girl Yolanda and walk about a mile and a half to some friend's house he knew. Sue would be upset while looking for her baby wondering where he had gone. Later that evening he would return home. That would just spoil everybody's Sunday. Sue didn't deserve that.

One Sunday while visiting Mrs. Reed; Dave walked down the street to a bar. He came back drowsy and had a headache. His mom said someone slipped a Mickey on him. She put a cool compress on his forehead, Dave laid on the sofa and slept it off. When he woke up, he was fine. Mrs. Reed told him to stay away from that bar.

When we were growing up, if you needed stitches mothers or grandmothers would use different remedies. They would clean the wound with hydrogen peroxide, apply mercurochrome, and a dressing. Some parents would use needles and thread. It seemed to work, but most of all God was watching over us.

My husband's good friend Jack was seeing Jane. They got married. They would come over or we would go to their house. We would make pizza, play cards, and drink beer. When Jack drank a beer or two he would tell all his business. That was funny.

I found out from Nita, that Jill is carrying a baby for Dave my husband. Six months later I was pregnant. I just wanted to send a message that I was the wife.

We were renting a small house with one bedroom. Now that I was pregnant we would have to find a bigger house with a bedroom for the baby. We started looking and found a two-bedroom house. The two-bedroom house was $30.00 more a month. We could afford that. We moved out of the smaller house into the larger house. We set up the nursery, baby bed, and all the essential things. I pulled out my sewing machine; I made lots of drawstring gowns.

I was walking in the bedroom and water squirted out of me on the floor. My water bag had burst; I wasn't in pain, so I called out to Dave. He grabbed my suitcase which was already packed. He drove me to the hospital.

While at the hospital, I started having labor pains. I was given an enema, shaved and an IV was started.

I delivered a baby boy weighing 6 pounds and 19 inches. Dave seemed to be attached to his son. He seemed to be enjoying fatherhood.

A year later, the landlord wanted to sell that house we were in. He gave us first preference, we didn't want to buy that house. The house was old; the house had been there since I was a child. Even though it had been renovated, we started looking again. This time we found a three-bedroom house next door to the Land Lord. For the first three months, everything was fine. Then the fourth month, the couple we were renting from started fighting. They would bring the fight outside while running around both houses; she would chase him with a gun. I had my child and was afraid of a bullet coming into the house. I was saving now for a down payment on a house. We started looking for land to purchase and build. We found land to purchase, got a builder, and looked at the different styles they built. Dave and I agreed on one. The builder started building. It took longer than ever to finish building our house; it snowed that year; something we rarely get down here in the South. Finally, in April we were ready to move in. I thought if I had to live another month with the fighting Land Lords, I would have a nervous breakdown. I didn't care who moved in after me. Also, the Land Lord had a son who was writing on my trash can, things I wouldn't repeat. I didn't say anything about the writing on the trash can because he would have denied it.

Once we got settled into our house, we made a vegetable garden every summer. Dave would tilt the soil and I would plant the seeds. He loved tomatoes so he would plant tomatoes, cucumbers, okra, and snapped beans. I loved doing that because it was relaxing. I was brought up with a garden. My Mom loved shelling fresh peas. She had one bowl and I had the other bowl shelling peas.

My friend Jane gave birth to a girl. As couples, we went out to restaurants, movies, and a club or two.

As my son grew, I got wind that he started bringing the child with him to different women's houses. Of course, I confronted him and he denied it. He got so involved with Helen that he left home and asked me for a divorce. I got an attorney and filed for a legal separation; at that time, you had to wait six months to get a legal separation and a year for a divorce. One of us had to move out of the house. My son and I moved in with my parents.

CHAPTER 11:
TIRED

———————

I started dating a guy named Tyrone who was divorced and had two children. He was a hard-working guy. He didn't seem to be a run-around guy. We went out to the movies, talked on the phone, and visited each other. Nothing clicked with that relationship. It was more of a friendship.

CHAPTER 12:

THE SEPARATION

B y the time six months had arrived, he had begged his way back home. Dave had brought all kinds of papers from his job for me to sign as beneficiary and I forgave him and took him back. Dave bought his way back home.

I got pregnant again and had another baby boy. They were five and a half years apart. Everything was going well, so I guess he kept everything quiet. He didn't want me to work but to be a stay home mom. I guess he figured out I would hear gossip about him if I worked.

My neighbor Jackie lived down the street from me and she would stop by and keep me company. She was a stay-at-home mom too. She had two boys. Her husband was a quiet man. Dave didn't like her at all. Dave said he saw her getting in a car with another man in the mall parking lot.

My sister-in-law Sue, found out that her husband Kenny was having an affair. She found a tricycle and other toys in the trunk of Kenny's car that didn't belong to their child. She found out this was for a lady named Amber's child, and Dave had been having an affair with her too.

Sue and Kenny's marriage survived that affair with Amber, but the marriage couldn't survive the fighting and she had had enough, her mother Mrs. Reed, had more than enough. Mrs. Reed called her cousin Annie in San Francisco and asked her to allow Sue and her two girls to stay with her until she got on her feet. Annie said yes. Sue purchased her bus ticket and left town when Kenny was at work.

Kenny was in for a surprise when he got home from work; no Sue or the girls.

Kenny used to just jump on Sue for anything. She didn't know what she had done to cause him to start hitting her. Sue used to cook every day, keep her house clean, and keep herself and the girls clean. It seemed like anything would spark a flame. If Kenny was mad with someone else it seemed Sue was his punching bag. Kenny tried to get her back by building her a new house. Sue found out about the new house, which was across the street from her mom. Kenny had told people he had built that house for Sue. That didn't make Sue come back to him. Sue and the girls would come out to visit her mom and go back to San Francisco.

While living in San Francisco, Sue met a young man. They had a son together. That relationship ended.

Kenny stopped trying to get her back due to the fact Sue had another man's child. Kenny lost the house he had built for Sue.

Kenny found himself another wife, but he didn't treat her well. He used her as a punching bag too. Her family hated him, but what can the family do if the person is not ready to leave? That lady ended up dying. Her family hated him even more.

Kenny got another wife. This was wife number 3. They had children together. She was a petite woman. Kenny didn't fight this woman. Matter of fact, he was afraid of her.

One day I had to go to the DMV to renew my driver's license. I pulled my number. I saw Kenny sitting there waiting to be called. He had that embarrassed look on his face when he saw me. I was embarrassed too. He looked so unkempt we talked for a short time. The look on his face seemed as if he wanted the floor to open up and swallow him. The floor wasn't going to part for Kenny.

Later I found out wife number three had left Kenny. He was living in his parent's house.

28

We drove out to San Francisco. My son Drew was six months old at the time. Ron was five and a half. We were going to see Sue and the girls. Dave's sister Desi wanted to go too; she was bringing one child. It was a long ride from Louisiana to California. We shipped our luggage by bus. We left that Friday at 1:00 p.m. and arrived in San Francisco at 2:00 a.m. Sunday morning. At 10:00 a.m. that Sunday morning we went to the bus station to see have our luggage arrived. They told us to come back on Monday morning. I guess we made good time on the road; we arrived before the luggage.

Our first stop was in Fort Stockton, Texas. On the second stop; we slept in Phoenix, Arizona. I was impressed we met a track star while traveling through Phoenix. No problem with our air conditioner while driving through the desert. A lot of people were having air conditioning problems. There were policemen out there to help the people who needed help.

We stayed out there for a week. When we got ready to leave Dave's sister Desi said she was going back on the bus. Desi was mad with Dave because they agreed to split the gas expense. Desi didn't think Dave was being fair with her. Desi had called Mrs. Reed and informed her about the situation and asked her mom for bus fare to return home. I didn't get into that because it was between a brother and a sister.

While out there in San Francisco I had a good time; I think we all had a good time despite the differences.

Sue had friends who would pick up the slack. Each night one of her friends would invite us over; we play cards and they would prepare a dinner for us. Everybody was nice.

We went to the San Diego Zoo, Oakland, Lombard Street in San Francisco's most crooked street, Fishman Warf, and while riding on the Golden Gate Bridge we looked over at Alcatraz. The weather was nice; while out there we had light jackets on in June.

I was enjoying some Lionel Richie and the Commodore Sweet Love while in San Francisco. I enjoyed myself; but, I was getting homesick. We left out that Monday morning. Ron was ok. Drew got fussy, he wasn't feeling good. He develops diarrhea. We had to get off the interstate and find a store to get medication for him. Dave was the driver; I was caring for the baby; Dave didn't want it any other way. Desi helped him drive there, but now she was returning on the bus. I think Desi agreed to split half of the gas but wanted Dave to exempt her. We finally made it home after being on the road for two days.

I grew up fishing with my dad. I was an only child for eleven and a half years. After marrying Dave, we went fishing a couple of times. Dave didn't care for fishing; Dave said waiting on a bite you may or may not get. Dave always suggested going to the fish market; his saying was a sure catch every time. I guess he was right in a sense. His other saying was work, work; don't let work, work you.

Dave was a good cook. We had flounder and red snapper in the freezer. Dave would prepare flounder with shrimp stuffing. Sometimes he would trick me into eating something that I wouldn't normally eat. He would tell me later when I finished eating that it was deer sausage.

I remember growing up my mom would cook all kinds of weird dishes and didn't tell you until you had finished eating. Me and my friend ate what she had cooked; I thought it was scrambled eggs with green onions we had it over hot rice; it was very good my friend even asked for seconds. When we finished eating I asked my mom what she had prepared? She answered, "Cow brain mixed with scrambled eggs." My mom was very tricky with her meals; I think it was rubbing off on Dave.

I was driving downtown while waiting at the red light to change. I saw a long blue Delta 88 Oldsmobile passing on the main street with a woman sitting in the front seat next to the door; Dave was driving; the woman had a large roller in her hair looking straight ahead. When he got home I asked him who was that woman in the car with you? he said, that was my sister. I didn't question it anymore I knew there was no truth in that. Dave would lie for no reason at times. When he starts sniffing when he's talking to you; you know that would be lies. You think she would have been sitting really close to him instead of next to the door. All things come to the light. Sometimes you may not find out who, what, or when but eventually you get an answer to your questions when you least expect it.

Most of my friends were older Ladies. I would ask them questions regarding my marriage situation. They would give me good advice. Their concerns were the money. They would always say to cook for Dave, wash his clothes, and perform your wifely duties. Let him play don't worry about that. That was a generation gap; the younger woman didn't feel like dealing with all of that. Older ladies always had this saying you can't measure arms with a man.

Dave had a cleaning company. I found out that was his side piece in the car with him when he said it was his sister. She was helping him clean his office building one night. I had some friends on the police force who told me the police were called because someone thought it was a break-in at the office that they were cleaning, and it was Dave and her in there. It had to be clarified by the office Manager that they were there cleaning up.

CHAPTER 13:

A BIG DISAPPOINTMENT

Three and a half years later I had another baby this time a girl this completed my family. I went into labor. He brought me to the hospital for every delivery, but this last one was different. When he got me to the hospital they wheeled me into the labor room and got me all set up. The nurse asked, "Where is your husband? We have paged him to come to the delivery room, and we have looked for him, but we can't find him." After the baby was born Dave did show up; I told him the nurse was looking for you; his reply was he went to Waffle House to eat, he was hungry. I just brushed it off senseless.

CHAPTER 14:

KEEPING YOUR MARRIAGE TOGETHER

In those days people, didn't believe in divorce and it was okay for a wife to accept what her husband did. Well of course the cheating started all over again, it probably never stopped. Each time I find out Dave is having an affair he tries to be more careful. Living in a small town where everyone knows everybody being more careful doesn't work.

I injured my back lifting on heavy things because he was working offshore in Texas. I tried to do everything myself I didn't like asking anyone else to do anything for me. He was out there seven days and off seven; usually, he would leave on the evening of day six. Dave would drive back to Texas and sleep nearby. Early in the morning they would be flown out to the platform by helicopter and let down on the platform.

One of Dave's co-worker missed the platform and fell into the gulf; he came up so fast that his wallet didn't have a chance to get wet.

Women would be calling him on our house phone which I had a private number; hanging up the phone in my face. I would get discussed at times, but soon forget. At times, he would try to get cleverer with some of his cheating, and other times I guess he didn't care or you might say careless with his love affairs. He knew my weakness was money and jewelry. He would have the floral shops deliver flowers, buy earrings and he would not cash his checks that were for the house. He would work a second job for his money.

CHAPTER 15:

DAVE IN THE HOSPITAL

———————•———————

Dave's right lung collapsed; he had to have a chest tube put in. While in the hospital Dave's women were calling and asking me questions and when I asked who was calling she said a friend. I gave Dave the phone. A nurse brought some flowers to Dave she said someone had left them at the nurse station. Dave looked at the flowers, the note, said from Bea. I had no idea who that was, or was it a fake name? He didn't want the flowers on the nightstand. He wanted them on top of his closet out of site. On top of the closet, you could barely see them. I tried to be nice while he was in the hospital. But, once he got home all hell broke loose. I didn't bite my tongue I let him have it. I would have that look in my eyes that I might do anything and he didn't trust that. He was fearful, but soon forgot. His lung collapsed two more times I stayed with him as a dedicated wife.

I had to bring Dave to New Orleans for procedures on his lungs. I would have worked twelve hours' night gone home got ready to bring Dave there to the Pulmonologist, which was an hour and twenty minutes depending on the traffic. I worked from 6:00 p.m. to 6:00 a.m. I would be so sleepy I would fall asleep in the waiting room. When I woke everybody would be looking at me. If they only knew.

Dave ended up having surgery. He did well in his recovery period.

CHAPTER 16:

DAVE WANTING TO CHANGE

D ave knew I preferred to be married to a Christian man so he would attend church every Sunday, and go to choir rehearsal every Monday evening if he wasn't working. He even went as far as studying to become a Lay Leader. Dave even asked me to ride with him some evenings to New Orleans to his Lay Leader class. He did complete Lay Leader got his certificate and delivered messages on Sundays when the Minister was out of town or special events.

I wanted to join the choir at church, but Dave didn't want me to join, Dave told me to just be a layman and watch the children. I would participate in the Christmas play with the children. The children would be on programs every third Sunday of the month. I enjoyed seeing the children participating. The children would do bible verses, sing, or perform skits. For the Christmas play, I played Mary in a stable with baby Jesus in a manger. Dave would be one of the wise men bearing gifts for baby Jesus. One of the church members would be the narrator.

I had to get ready on Sunday for church and dress three small children. I had to cook on Sundays either before we went to church or after we got back from church. I would get up at 4:00 a.m. on Sunday if I was going to cook before church. I liked my food fresh; that's why I didn't cook on Saturday night and refrigerate and warm up the next day.

We had family and friend day once a year. I enjoyed inviting my family and friends. All the members would bring a covered dish after the service everyone ate and talked. People you hadn't seen in years were there. Some family members came from different parts of the United States.

One of the Members of the trustee board must have been paying attention to Dave; he commented on Dave coming to church alone.

He continues to see other women. He thought I didn't know anything. So good so far, I guess he thought.

CHAPTER 17:
OVERWORKED

I had physical therapy for a ruptured disc, pills, and injections, but nothing seemed to help so I ended up having surgery. The next day after surgery the phone in the room started ringing; it was hard for me to answer the phone I was on pain medication for the pain I was in; I had a drainage tube in my back. I was finally able to reach the phone and when I could pick up the phone I said hello they just held on and then hung up I guess they were expecting Dave to answer. That hurts I could read between the lines. I was a person who didn't hold grudges I forgave and forget. I would pay him back by fantasizing about an affair while lying in bed next to Dave.

Dave had another business he started; his painting company. He closed his cleaning service. He was doing well. His full-time job was as an operator at a plant. He was a good provider for his family. Not a family man. You might say a family man with a teenage mind. The question is how long will I wait for Dave to mature?

Some women are good at ignoring them and just going on with their lives while their husbands are leaving every row upturn. That's hard for me. I entered this relationship with the idea of respect for each other, honesty, a feeling of safety, friendship, trust, loyalty, and fairness. I just want to look up to my spouse; I want him to be my hero, my knight in shining armor, and a strong sense of morality.

CHAPTER 18:

WHERE IS THE RESPECT?

———————●———————

While we were visiting Dave's mom Mrs. Reed one Sunday his two brothers were sitting on the porch. They wanted Dave to sit out there with them and smoke marijuana with them. Dave didn't approve of that so, he came into the house and told me. We left and headed home.

CHAPTER 19:

DAVE FINDING A SISTER HE DIDN'T KNOW EXISTED

D ave found a sister whom he never knew existed. She was a sweet young Lady. Sonia would come out and see Dave and me and we would go see her. Sonia was his Dad daughter. I remember one Easter I was sick and was discharged from the hospital. Dave called Sonia; she came out and took care of me and the children. Sonia got their baskets ready for Easter and cooked our Easter dinner.

CHAPTER 20:

A DISTURBING VISIT

D ave and I went to visit his Mom Mrs. Reed. While at her house my sister-in-law, Rose called and sacked her out about her husband Brad, Mrs. Reed's son. Mrs. Reed lets Brad bring other women to her house while being married to Rose and holds them a better conversation than the daughter-in-law. Mrs. Reed told Rose I can't do anything about that. I thought this is your house you don't want to do anything about it.

Brad was just from one woman to the other. He didn't stay long with Rose; only to come and make another baby and leave her again. He wasn't even there for the birth of the babies. Rose just kept taking him back and having more babies.

Other women had babies for Brad too. Brad worked once a year in grinding or if anything he would stay with women that would take care of him.

Dave was not compared to his brother Brad when it comes to providing for his family. Brad wanted the women to take care of him.

CHAPTER 21:

THE ONE TIME I SAW MRS. REED GET ON BRAD'S CASE

———◆———

The one time I saw Mrs. Reed get angry with Brad was after Liz, a lady he was living with had died. Brad liked Liz. He had left Rose again and moved in with Liz. She was 5'6" tall and weighed about 110 pounds. She had a baby girl for him. Liz started having headaches, ended up having an aneurysm, and died at 23 years old. She left a baby behind. Liz's sister stepped up to the plate to raise the baby. Rose, Brad's wife acknowledged the baby Brad had with Liz, and was willing to raise the baby with her children. Rose was a stronger woman than I could have ever been.

Funeral arrangements were made for Liz. The Night of the wake

Brad went to a motel with another woman. After the funeral service, Mrs. Reed got on Brad about his conduct. Brad said he needed someone to help him with his grief. I was stunned. Where were his morals? Do to others as you would have them do to you. Luke 6:31 NIV. It seemed he was all about himself.

CHAPTER 22:

WHAT'S AHEAD?

———————•———————

B rad and Rose had seven kids. He went back to Rose for a short time after Liz's death. Brad left again; he met a woman in New Orleans, Louisiana, and was planning on moving in with her. Brad was driving out of New Orleans on his way back home to get his clothes to stay with that woman when he lost control of his truck and flipped it over a couple of times. Someone traveling behind him alerted 911. He was brought to the Emergency Room. Brad was admitted to the trauma unit for about a month, then later transferred to Jackson, Mississippi to a rehabilitation hospital. Brad became a quadriplegic. While in the rehabilitation hospital, all his women were coming to see him. The women didn't care if his wife was there or not. Then Brad asked Dave to check to see what happened to the truck that caused it to flip over. Dave found that nothing was wrong with the truck; everything was intact. It wasn't raining, the road was dry, there were no tire blowouts, no steering problem and he hadn't been drinking. Brad was puzzled. The old saying "every road has an end."

When Brad was discharged from the rehabilitation hospital in Mississippi, his wife took him home. She was a better woman than me because I would have put him in the nursing home.

Rose had to feed, bathe, and turn him over every two hours while he was in bed. Getting him up in the wheelchair was a lot for her to take on. Only one of their sons said he would help; the other sons said they weren't going to help because he never did anything for them.

Rose and her son Bill did what they could for Brad; he was so demanding about sitting up for long hours that they just let him sit as long as he wanted. I think she was afraid of him, even though he was in a wheelchair. The one good thing out of the deal; she got his disability check. Rose and Bill had to give total care. Feeding, bathing, giving medication, getting him out of bed, and putting Brad in his wheelchair, were a challenge.

Brad developed a wound on his butt due to sitting up for long hours and refusing to go to bed. He was hospitalized for wound care. While in the hospital, Brad started having hallucinations and was telling the workers where to find marijuana. Once the goal of care was reached, he was discharged home.

Once back home, from the hospital, he was back into his demanding role. Rose let him have his way. Brad ended up in the hospital again with extensive wound care, blood transfusion, and intravenous antibiotics. It was bad. This time, Brad didn't make it; he was septic.

Rose arranged Brad's death service well; Mrs. Reed didn't handle that well at all Brad, was her firstborn.

Mrs. Reed stayed in and out of the emergency room; nothing life-threatening. It just took time for her to heal from the loss of her son Brad. Parents prefer to be buried by their children rather than burying their children.

My mom had come over to visit us. We walked out of the family room. I wanted to show her some new drapery I had made for Crystal's room. My mom had left her purse in the family room on the floor. I walked back to the family room and caught Dave in my mom's purse. I guess he was looking for some of her medications. She was on anti-anxiety medication. It hurt me to see him doing that. I called out to my mom that I was back in the family room; my mom returned. Dave didn't get what he wanted because I wasn't moving. I never mentioned it. Why didn't he just ask her? Dave surely didn't mention that; he was busted.

Dave always says he lost his wedding band. He gave all kinds of excuses like; "to keep from losing my finger, I had to let the ring go." Of course, "I would purchase another one for him".

I always wanted to look nice, even when getting ready for bed at night I would put makeup on my face. I ended up getting cysts on the inside of my eyelids; upper and lower lids. I had to have them removed. I was so nervous when it was finished. I wanted to get up, but my legs wouldn't move. The procedure went well. I didn't feel any pain. I guess it was because I was awake. I even frightened the staff. I drank a soft drink, talked with the staff, relaxed, and then left.

I never went to bed with make-up again. If someone loves you it shouldn't matter.

My friend Jane had her problem too. She came to the house crying because Jack had left her and she wanted Dave to talk to Jack; not knowing that Dave probably knew everything before it happened. Jack had gotten so involved with this woman, that he left home, got an apartment, and got one of his family members to share an apartment with him. Dave promised Jane he would talk to him. She found out he left her for one of his co-workers. Jack must have been gone for about two months before he finally returned home. Jane took him back; she wanted her marriage to work. I guess it took time for the relationship to heal. She got pregnant and had another girl. The relationship seemed to be going well, but Jack got involved again and left home again. When he decided to return home, the relationship was never the same; no trust was there. They finally ended up getting a divorce. I was just devastated. I didn't know what to do. I was feeling like getting a divorce too to prove my loyalty to them. Jack didn't waste any time in remarrying. My husband Dave was at the wedding as the best man. Our Daughter was in the wedding as a junior bridesmaid because Jack was her godfather. We left that Friday for rehearsal and the rehearsal dinner. I told Jane I would give her all the information about the wedding when I got back. Jane wanted to get back with him, but he was determined to marry this woman Debra who was twenty-nine years younger. He didn't want Jane anymore. He said she was having an affair when they were married. I wondered who drove her to that.

We left that Friday because we had to drive to Alexandria, Louisiana which was one hour and thirty minutes, depending on the traffic. We had to check into the hotel and then head to practice. We met at the wedding party. I didn't think much. After the practice, the wedding party had a dinner at the bride's house because the groom lived an hour and a half away. Everybody was friendly and the food was good. I met my mom's first cousins there; the bride's dad was also my mom's first cousin. Small world. I only knew Bertha who lived in Grayville, Louisiana. She would go to my mom's all the time and visit with her and her boyfriend, who her children didn't approve of. She was a widow. I think she deserved to have a friend. Most of the time her family tried to dictate for her like she was a Child. Bertha kept going out with Ben and didn't let her family control her.

Saturday, the day of the wedding went smoothly and started on time. It was a rainbow wedding. The groomsmen were dressed in black tuxes. After the wedding, Dave told me he was going to drive the groom's car and the bride's sister was going to ride with him to the reception, so I said okay. Later at the reception, he came to me and said the bride's sister wanted him to drive her to the house to get more liquor. I didn't question it. They didn't stay long. I saw that they had made it back. Later, she brought her camera over and started talking to him. We were standing together so she asked me if I could take a picture of him and her together. I was wondering what in the hell was going on. Yes, I did take the pictures because I was trying to be nice in front of other people. The bride's sister was named Camille. Camille started dancing on the floor alone, beckoning Dave to come dance with her. He shrugged it off; the third time she beckoned him he went on the dance floor. He never could dance worth a damn; he had two left feet. I was ready to go home, but my son and daughter were having fun and weren't ready to go home. I was miserable and mad as hell. I was in her territory. I couldn't say anything because I didn't know any of those people. I had to hold my peace. Camille's stepfather came over, introduced himself, and asked me what was my relationship with Dave. I said I was his wife and he asked again and I said Dave's wife. So, what was Dave telling people? I found out Camille's stepfather was my mom's first cousin; two sister's children. My grandmother died when my mom was nine years old and left six children. My grandfather reared them by himself with the help of the oldest child who helped to watch the smaller ones. He never remarried. After my grandmother died, her sisters wanted to split the children up and take one each. My grandfather wasn't having it.

I had so much to tell Jane when I got back, but nothing about Jack. It was about me and Dave, how I was disrespected at the wedding, and how pissed off I was.

Jane found out Jack had been seeing Debra for at least two years when they were together. Jack would've said it was all Jane's fault. Jack had to find someone else to blame other than himself.

Jack and his new bride got an apartment in Baton Rouge. I paid all the bills so I started noticing the telephone bill like how many times Dave was calling Jack's house within a day. Was he calling Jack and Jack was putting him in a three-way conversation? I didn't even question him. I was just letting him have all the rope he needed to hang himself.

On Saturday evening my phone rang. When I answered a woman's voice on the other end said she was calling from a law firm in California and was trying to get in touch with Dave. What Law firm was going to be calling a client on Saturday evening? See, Dave had told this woman that he had a lawsuit pending from working with asbestos when he was living in California. I guess they had a date or she just wanted to see him. She had some nerve. That's low on Dave's part.

I was scheduled to work at Memorial Hospital on Sunday. Dave got up, went to church came home, changed clothes, and left. I kept waiting on him to return home to keep the children; so, I could go to work. I called Jack's number and asked him if Dave was there and he said no. For some reason, I didn't believe him. I called my job and told them I was ill and wouldn't be able to come in that night. I called my friend Jane; Jack's ex-wife to find out Jack's address. She gave me the address. Jane said she would ride with me so I went to her house and picked her up.

We went to Baton Rouge, found his apartment, and guess whose truck I saw at Jack's apartment? Dave's truck. Jane didn't want Jack to see her so I drove to a store over on the next street and let her out to wait until I came back. I drove back over to Jack's apartment. I knocked on the door and Jack answered the door. I asked him why he had told me Dave wasn't there. He was speechless. I walked passed him and saw Dave in the kitchen. I didn't see Camille; I guess she was hiding. I told him he needed to keep the kids because I had to work that day. He didn't take long to get home behind me. I guess I rained on his parade. I went back to the store over on the next street to pick up Jane. I told her what happened and she laughed. She said she wished she was a fly on the wall when I went to Jack's apartment. Dave told me that Jack said he could've pressed charges on me for coming to his apartment. I guess that was a threat. Why didn't he press charges? Jack was my daughter's godfather.

When Dave wasn't working on Sundays he would dress up and go to church alone; that's right alone. He didn't wait for his family so we rode in separate cars. He said we were too slow. Dave never helped to get the boys ready for church. After Church was over, he would come home and change clothes. Dave would get his friend Mike to come over and they would say they were going to dirt bike races. They never said where the dirt bike races were, but that's cool. I just did my normal Sunday, cooked fed the children, and later went to my parents' house.

Mike's wife Vera, found a woman's picture in his truck. Another weekend she found a television and more in his truck, like he was helping this woman to move. Vera found her telephone number, made a phone call to her, and told her Mike was her husband. She told her to leave Mike alone and even kept the woman's television. I am sure she knew he was married. That woman must have gotten afraid because she left Mike alone.

My sister Lynn would stay with my kids. While I worked from 6:00 p.m. to 6:00 a.m., Dave was working offshore. When he was home, he would get my sister to keep the kids so he could go places. Lynn would think it was for a short time because he would call and tell her he was on his way, was crossing the bridge, or sometimes say he had trouble with his truck. He would just be coming home after 5:00 a.m. when I was getting off at 6:00 a.m. That became a regular thing. It was okay to use me, but I was not going to stand for him using my family.

I was at work one night when my co-workers and I were talking, when out of the blue, the security officer, Will, started talking about his life. He said when he was in the military, his wife was pregnant. Will said he wanted to surprise his wife, but he was surprised. She was in their bed with another man. Will said he called a taxi. When the taxi arrived, he picked up his luggage and left, but before he left, he told the guy you better treat her right. He stayed overnight at his sister's house and the next day he went back to the military where he was stationed. His mom and sister talked to him about staying with his wife to raise his children. Will said he went back to her, but he just couldn't stay with her.

The house supervisor wanted to share her story. She said she was a charge nurse at a hospital in Mississippi. Her husband, Steve was ill. Steve had home health workers who came to care for him. She came home early one day and found Steve and the home health nurse in bed. Rachel said she walked out of the house; got in her car, and got the police to escort her for her belongings. Rachel said Steve had fooled her.

I guess that was a message from God. My co-workers told their stories and my story was next.

Dave changed jobs again. He got tired of working offshore in Texas. He transferred to a plant in Alabama.

I was unhappy; whenever I was away from home I was happy. When I was on my way home I was okay, but when I turned down my street to go home I was saddened. I hated going home because it wasn't a home anymore; it was a house.

Our oldest son, Ron started going to college in Alabama. Dave had been trying to convince me to get an apartment in Alabama. His excuse was that the guys he was staying with were too nasty. All these men worked for the same company; the day shift and night shift employees. I knew he only wanted an apartment so that he could bring women there. So, Dave ended up getting Ron an apartment for college. He moved in with Ron. Ron didn't have weekend classes so he would come back to Louisiana on weekends. Dave worked seven days on and seven days off. He was at the apartment every other weekend.

Whenever I went to Ron and Dave's apartment, I would look in the kitchen cabinets. I saw two zodiac sign drinking glasses; one said Sagittarius and the other said Virgo. Then I found papers for a cruise. I was shocked. I thought he was planning a cruise; not once did I think it was for me. While I was at the apartment, the phone started ringing. I answered the phone and I could hear people in the background. A woman asked to speak to a name I didn't know. As I have learned the other woman always knows the wife while the wife is always the last to find out who the other woman is.

Dave worked every other weekend. On weekends Ron would come home. On Sunday nights or sometimes on Mondays, Ron would go back depending on his class schedule for that semester.

I went to the apartment with my daughter Crystal I found a prescription bottle with the name, Mike Ben on it. I asked Crystal if she knew Mike Ben; Crystal said, yes that was Mike, a friend of Daddy. When Ron wasn't up there on weekends Dave must have been really rowdy.

He came home that Friday and told me that the electricity was turned off. The utility company was going to put it on Saturday, so he had planned on going back Saturday morning. That was strange to me; even though I was in another state, I thought you would have to wait until Monday. He left that Saturday morning and headed back to Mobile, Alabama. Saturday, I told my daughter to pack her bags; we would go surprise her dad. It was a three-hour drive. It was dark; the sun had gone down when I got to the apartment. I wasn't sure if he was there. I parked the car. I got the flashlight out just in case the lights were not on. When I got to the door, I put the key in and unlocked the door, but the night chain was on. My hands were small, so I slid my hand in between the door and door frame, unlocked the night chain then proceeded to turn on the light. To my surprise, there was light. It was very quiet. I walked to the bedroom and I saw two people sleeping in bed. I was stunned and started to write in the mirror "Lisa was here," but instead I went to bed and said, "Oh it's you," "Camille!!" My cousin, Camille said, "I am not your cousin." That was when I hit her a few times with the flashlight I had in my hand. I guess with the bed bouncing up and down, he woke up, saw me, and jumped out of bed in his birthday suit. I told my daughter to leave the room. I was surprised, but I shocked the hell out of him.

Camille jumped out of bed in her birthday suit and grabbed his robe off the wall I had seen that robe figured a woman had purchased it for him because he wasn't going to buy that. She locked herself in the bathroom. I tried to get the door open, but I couldn't. I told my daughter to come with me to call the police. The phone was off in the apartment; he had not paid the bill. While riding down the street I saw the police at a convenience store. I told them what happened. The officer told me not to fight. I would go to jail, so I agreed not to. They followed me back to the apartment to talk to him. She was not in the apartment. She had either left, was hiding, or was at a neighbor's house. The police told us to talk. He said if he had followed his first mind, I would have never caught him. He also said he wasn't thinking with the correct head, he was thinking with his other head. I went into the drawers looking for her clothes. I bagged them up and put them in the trash bin next to the apartment. Later, I saw Dave getting her clothes out of the trash bin and putting them in his truck. That was when I knew it was a losing cause. I left and drove my three hours back to Louisiana. He wasn't long behind me. He came into the house and sat on the sofa looking exhausted. I didn't want to talk, so he hung around for a while and said he wasn't staying there that night. I might kill him. Dave said he was going to stay with his mom. I doubted that. It didn't matter to me anymore. I was done. I called my pastor and told him what I had found. The pastor said, "You can forgive him and take him back, but whatever you do tell your children what you are going to do." I called my children to my bedroom, and they sat on the bed. I told them I was filing for a divorce and they were quiet. Later, I found out the boys had seen him making telephone calls. I caught him that Saturday night. There was nothing I could do on Sunday. Monday morning, I called an attorney and made an appointment that day. I told my attorney what happened. My attorney filed for a divorce. I found out the attorney Dave had, was from another town, someone Camille knew from her hometown. Dave told all his friends he had caught me with a man and he was divorcing me in six months. I divorced Dave in nineteen days. He remained bitter because he got caught. He said I should have killed him.

I was so hurt I kept saying "The apartment, the apartment." I was picking up an extra shift to help pay for the apartment. My attorney told me to forget about that apartment. She had to jog my memory. My attorney said, "You are a lady, Lisa." Camille is a woman. I felt good about that.

I packed up all of Dave's clothes. I took his mom's picture off the wall and packed it up. I grabbed the bag that he takes to work and found three wedding bands that he pretended to have lost. I had believed him. I just shook my head in disbelief. He didn't want to be married. I was giving him what he wanted. I should have divorced him a long time ago. Dave would always say to me "Let nobody set asunder." I guess that was his way of brainwashing me. I fell for it hook, line, and sinker.

When he came by to pick up his belongings he saw his mom's picture in the box off the wall. He repeated three times "That's mother picture." I don't know what he expected, we were starting a new life. I said, "I thought you would want your mom's picture". He was just stunned.

I had so many problems. I thought if I smoked it would help. I went to the store and purchased a pack of cigarettes. I put the cigarettes in my purse, which lasted over a year. I never learned to inhale or could even stand the smell of tobacco. I gave that up.

At one time, I looked forward to celebrating our 50th wedding anniversary, but I just couldn't take it anymore. I guess Dave never thought the choices he had made, had consequences.

I had a lot of sleepless nights before the divorce waiting for Dave to come home. The bars close at 2:00 a.m. Where are you, Dave? I had nightmares, and all kinds of thoughts running through my mind. There were rumors on the street and old classmates were calling my mom asking her if Dave's girlfriend killed me. Different ones were calling her to give their condolences. She told them it was not true and I was very much alive. It had to be disturbing to my mom.

CHAPTER 23:

LIFE GOES ON

———————•———————

We were divorced and I didn't have to deal with all of that anymore. I was thankful that God had seen me through the trials and tribulations.

Ron was still in college. I dropped him off. I would purchase food for the apartment. Sometimes Ron would be so hurt that he called me crying, saying his dad had brought Camille and her children there and they ate all the food. I would have to turn around and go back and buy more food. I remember when Dave was furnishing the apartment, he told me a friend had given him the furniture. He had me sewing the busted pillows for the sofa. I was in good spirits sewing and sewing. When I was sitting on the sofa waiting on Ron I dropped my keys on the side of the sofa. I stuck my hand on the side of the sofa. I found some old papers for

Camille dated five or six years ago, with her address on them. I was in a reality shock. All along it was Camille's furniture I was repairing. I thought about Johnny Taylor's song, "Everything's Out in the Open".

Did Dave have a conscience? You would think Dave would've been tired of slipping and hiding in life. No matter where you, go someone you know will see you.

I couldn't believe I thought I knew Dave, but it turned out I didn't know Dave at all. I thought this was not the man I had married. Dave just didn't show his true colors until after we were married. How long was I willing to wait for a change? We, as women always, think we can change a man. The only thing changing about a man is his clothes. You have a choice live with it or don't live with it.

At one time, I had considered moving out of state, putting the house up for sale, and buying another one out there. So, Dave wouldn't have to travel back and forth. I even applied for a nursing license for that state and got it. I prayed about the situation and looked to God for answers. Then, I found Dave in bed with another woman. Where I had considered moving. That was my answer. I no longer wanted him.

Women take relationships seriously. Most men, I'm not going to say all, are not serious.

He came around after the divorce trying to talk. I didn't give him time to talk because when I wanted to talk, he wasn't ready. I had even suggested we get a marriage counselor when we were having problems before the divorce. He didn't want one. He always said he didn't want anybody in his business, telling him what to do. He didn't think it was necessary.

After the divorce, my cousin Ricky came over to talk to me. We were more like sister and brother instead of cousins. My grandmother raised him. We stayed next door to my grandmother. She was my dad's mother. Ricky didn't want me to get hurt anymore. He knew what I had been going through. He just told me "You know you got your house". Ricky said, "Some men just looking for somewhere to stay beware". Some of them looking for you to take care of them. My other cousin, Lawrence, said, "You finally woke up." We were a close-knit family. Dave had always told me, "Nobody wants you or you not going to find anybody." That was Dave's way of making me feel insecure and lowering my self-esteem. I heard what Dave was saying, but I never doubted myself. That was a form of brainwashing.

My cousin Nick called me to find out what Attorney I used, so he could use her as well. He wasn't happy in his marriage and hadn't been for years. They were in the house together in different bedrooms. Every other week Nick would call me. I had to give him words of encouragement. While in the other bedroom for years Nick had fallen in love with someone else. Nick's wife got upset, but what did she expect? She threw him to the wolves. Nick went through with his divorce and got re-married.

My mom and my sister were my greatest support. My sister Lynn said, "Don't you forget how he treated you." I will always remember what Lynn said, "I forgive Dave, but I will never forget."

Dave wanted his sister Sonia to talk to me to take him back, but she refused. She didn't want to get involved. He got angry with Sonia because she refused. Dave stopped talking to Sonia for quite some time. He went to a minister's wife, First Lady Mary, and talked to her. Dave asked First Lady Mary to talk to me. She called me and we talked. First Lady Mary even called my mom and talked to her. My mom would tell me what she and First Lady Mary talked about. She explained the importance of staying together even if you must sleep in different bedrooms. I didn't want to live like that just for the children. I didn't think living in those kinds of arrangements or vibes was healthy.

My children were having a hard time dealing with the divorce. I had to get counseling for Drew and Crystal. Crystal didn't want to be with her friends whose parents were together. Crystal started making friends with children of single parents. I knew the healing process would take time. I knew we weren't the only ones to go through this.

I got up and got ready for church. I was hoping I wouldn't see Dave at church. If he was going to continue his membership there then I was going to find another church to attend. All the children had been Christian and Baptist there. I had been through too much with Dave. I just wanted a fresh start. I didn't think that was too much to ask. Dave must have felt the same way I felt.

Dave joined the church where First Lady Mary was a member. On Sundays, the members said he would start crying so badly they had to bring him out of church for a while, to calm him down. About a month later, the members said he started bringing a woman named Camille and her son to church with him. The members thought that was his son, but First Lady Mary wanted me to take him back for the sake of the children, even if we had to sleep in different bedrooms. I didn't want to live like that. Just being in the house together. First Lady Mary would call me every week trying to get me to take him back.

My dad was ill and hoped we would get back together. My dad knew what his mom had to deal with when he was growing up. He saw his dad on Friday and not again until Monday. He didn't like that. It was very important to my dad that his girls get a proper education to be able to take care of themselves and not depend on a man to take care of them.

Dave was angry with my sister Lynn. The day we had to attend court to start the divorce proceeding, my attorney put my sister on the stand and questioned her. He didn't like her answers. He told me he could get my sister for perjury. I tuned him out. He was calling my parents' house and hanging up the phone when they answered. They knew it was him because the calling started after court.

I kept busy so I wouldn't think about the divorce. Dave would wait until it got dark to pass by the house every day. People in the neighborhood would see him driving through. The neighbors would tell me when they saw him riding in the neighborhood.

Our friends were divided. The guys would be on Dave's side and their wives would be on my side. I guess picking sides came naturally. Then Dave started borrowing money from his friends. Dave wouldn't repay his friends the money he borrowed from them, so his friends got mad with him and were on my side. One of his friends was ready to fight him. He had loaned him a large amount of cash and couldn't get it back. His friend was fighting mad. Dave was not a fighter. In elementary school, Dave would give his lunch money up to keep from fighting.

On the court date when we went for the divorce proceeding, the Judge asked Dave for an address to send his divorce papers. He said, "He didn't have an address". My attorney said, "Just give me an address to send your divorce papers".

After the divorce, Dave just started spiraling down. He wasn't getting along with some of his co-workers. He brought a gun on the job premises. Workers had been terminated for that before. The work handbook stated no firearm on the premises. Dave must have said he had his gun in his truck. They found Dave's gun. Dave went to arbitration but was not able to get his job back. Dave was just making all kinds of bad decisions. Maybe he couldn't handle the divorce.

I changed the locks on the doors. I had become an expert. I didn't have to pay anyone to change the locks anymore. I observed the first man when we were going through the legal separation "I said to myself this is easy I can do that." I learned how to light the central heating system and turn it off. I learned how to troubleshoot before calling someone to fix something.

Dave came by one evening to see if everything was ok. He walked around the house Dave brought it to my attention, that it had a cut on the bathroom screen window. I didn't get alarmed about it. I thought it probably was Dave's to scare me to take him back. I was not a glutton for punishment. I knew what I had been through and was not going to travel that road again.

One time Dave said he was going to a matinee to see the greyhounds run. For some reason, I called the track and was told the dogs had a virus and the track was shut down.

I thought about all the working out of state; was it legit? Dave told me, he had told his supervisor that if he had any overtime he was available. He got the call from his mobile to work from 11:00 p.m. until 7:00 a.m. His job is a three-hour ride. He asked me to drive him, so I brought Crystal with me. We dropped him off at work in Bayou La Batre. We had to find a hotel or motel to stay because it was after 11:00 p.m. Every motel we pulled up to had "no vacancy" on the door. We saw one hotel and I decided I would stop. The couple in front of me and Crystal got the last room. The manager said there was a big convention in town for the weekend. He said he had a friend who was a manager at a hotel on Highway 90. He called him and he had two rooms left. I gave him my name. He asked his friend to hold that room for me. The hotel was beautiful. Dave was getting off at 7:00 a.m. We checked out of the hotel and were over at the plant for 7:30 a.m. because they had to give a report. Dave was so full of tricks. I wondered "Did another woman pick him up when I dropped him off and brought him back when it was time to get off". It seems all his co-workers knew his business. Even when we went to his work parties some of the men would make wisecracks in front of me, like giving hints. I had a keen ear for reading between the lines.

Dave had some blood work done. Dave must have given my

number. The doctor's office called me with his lab and x-ray results. I told the nurse Dave and I were divorced. "Let me give you his mother's number where he can be reached." Why would Dave want me to know his results? I wouldn't want him to know my results.

Our oldest son, Ron, got married. Dave didn't come to the wedding. Me and my family attended along with the bride's family and friends. I didn't know if it bothered our son or not, but Ron was resentful toward him. He knew too much about him and his disrespectful ways. Sons are on their mother's side regardless and daughters are daddy girls.

I was single and divorced. I thought I would go out to the club. I asked several friends, but they all had other plans, weddings, going out of town and one was sick. So, I was determined to go out. I never went out alone before. I had to decide whether I was going to sit at the bar or a table. I just picked this club. I had never been there. It was so dark when I entered I stumbled to a table. My eyes finally adjust. I sat there for a while then the waiter came over to take my order; I ordered a beer. A guy named Barry came over and asked me to sit at the table with him. I said okay. I went over to his table. He introduced me to his brother Bobby and Bobby's girlfriend Rhonda. Barry seemed nice. Barry said he asked me over to his table so the guys wouldn't bother me.

Barry and I exchanged numbers. Barry was an older guy. Every Saturday night Barry and I went out to the clubs. Sometimes his brother Bobby and Rhonda would come out with us. The relationship between me and Barry grew.

Bobby and Rhonda got married. Barry and I continued to go out. I met the rest of Barry's family. My mom and sister met Barry. My mom didn't care for Barry. My sons liked Barry, my daughter never said whether she liked him or not.

I was kind of hooked on astrology. I was an Aries and Barry was Pisces with signs of the fish, which just slipped out of your hands. He wasn't a match for Aries. Pisces compatibility was Cancer and Scorpio. Aries compatibility was a Leo or Sagittarius. I had married Dave who was a Sagittarius.

Bobby told me Barry didn't have a Bible or even went to church. Barry and I attended lots of functions together. I was not interested in a commitment. I just wanted to go out and have fun because I had too much trauma with Dave and I couldn't stand the thought of reliving that.

If something broke at my house, Bobby would come over and fix it. Barry was a supervisor on his job. If I called or needed anything Barry would leave the job and come to my house.

Bobby worked in Barry's crew. Bobby said, "Lisa I am going to transfer because Barry works me too hard; he gives me the worst assignment." I asked Barry why he gave Bobby the worst assignment. Barry said he didn't want anybody to think he was playing favoritism. So of course, Bobby transferred and was happy after that.

Barry talked about how Bobby had been on drugs. Barry said the rest of the family had turned their backs on Bobby. Barry said he never turned his back on Bobby even when he was going through his crisis.

I told Barry about my experience with Dave at Camille's sister Debra's wedding. All the disrespect. Barry said I should have left him at the wedding and let him get home the best way he could.

Barry's brother Bill would be out every weekend with his girlfriend Jill. I started seeing Bill come out alone. Barry told me Jill found out she had breast cancer. Bill broke it off with Jill. Barry was upset with Bill. Barry said you just don't break it off with someone because they are sick. Barry was torn up about that situation. He said Bill needed to be there for Jill.

Some Saturday nights, we didn't go out. Barry had to babysit his two grandsons for his daughter if she had to work or go out of town. Barry's daughter Tammy was a beautiful girl.

I broke up with Barry because I was looking for someone to settle down with and not in the clubs every weekend. Barry was just someone that helped me to get through my divorce, but he wasn't the one I wanted to settle down with.

After I broke up with Barry, I heard he sold drugs. I was devastated. I had put myself in danger. I would never put myself in danger knowingly. I could recall when we were out at the bar, he had to go to the bathroom a lot. I didn't think much of that. One night while we were at the club Barry asked me why he had to go to the bathroom so much. I told Barry "You are drinking; you must have an overactive bladder and see the doctor you never know."

I always think good of people. I guess I judge people by myself with good intentions. I saw guys going into the bathroom, then he would go. I didn't know anything was going on. Barry must have been conducting his business.

Every time Dave came to the house to see the kids, one age fifteen and one twelve-year-old, he would park on the road at the end of the driveway. He always had a different woman in the truck every time he visited which was just a short time because someone was sitting in the truck waiting on him. What was all this about insecurity, showing off, or what?

Whenever Dave picked up Crystal, he would question her. Dave would ask her who was I seeing. And what was his name? What's the point? Crystal was a daddy's girl. She would go stay with him and Camille. Crystal would claim she was getting even. She would call me on their telephone, which was long distance plus she would call her friends and talk too. Crystal would run their phone bill up. They had to pay the bill. Sometimes the telephone would get disconnected. Daddy Dave didn't say a word. Camille's family said Camille was jealous of Crystal because whatever Crystal wanted, Dave would get it. Drew was fifteen years old. Drew was busy working and in school.

Dave and Camille brought the children out-of-state to an amusement park. Camille had three children and Dave had Crystal. Dave wouldn't pay for Camille's children he only paid for Crystal and himself to go into the park.

I started seeing Jerome after I broke up with Barry. When Jerome came over to see me I guess Dave would park on the side of the street and watch the house to see who was coming and going. Jerome said one night when he left, Dave followed him and put bright lights on him for miles. My children liked Jerome. He would cook for my family, and purchase a large flocked Christmas tree for Christmas. He was very generous when it came to money, but I had to find the one I was comfortable with. I was making a 99-degree turn. I wasn't looking for looks anymore. I was concerned about the way I was going to be treated. I want a man who feels secure, financially stable, not abusive verbally or physically, a Christian Man, and please a nonsmoker. One man I met I asked, do you smoke? his answer was "Yes, but I can quit". I said "No you can't," so that was ended before it got started.

It had gotten to the point where Dave was talking to my neighbor to go to court with him, so he could get custody of the children. I would have to pay him child support. My neighbor informed me and refused his suggestion. Dave had gotten fired from his operator job. Some of his customers are suing him regarding the paint jobs. His world seemed to be crumbling. He was bouncing from one low-paying job to another. He wasn't paying anything to the children. What the court had ordered for child support, I received only twice.

I worked two jobs to make ends meet after the divorce. I had so many bills. Dave wasn't even paying his truck note. They were calling me for his truck note. I said, "I can't pay that I have children to take care of and you can go pick it up". The finance company personnel said he thought he had seen the truck. On the front of the truck, he had his initials and his girlfriend's initials. I told him that was the one. It took the company that financed Dave's truck, one year to pick it up, with no payments. I told myself "Lisa only the strong survive." I had to put food on the table for my children and keep a roof over their heads. I wasn't about to pay all of Dave's bills.

My mom called me saying my dad was not looking good. She

wanted to call 911, but dad refused. I told her to call the ambulance anyway. When my mom got off the phone with me, she went into the bedroom. dad was not responding. My mom called 911. I guess Dad was tired and wanted to die. Mom called me from the hospital, and she said, "Come see your dad we are in the emergency room," not knowing he was dead. mom said when the paramedics came to bring my dad to the emergency room, he had a faint heartbeat.

The nurse asked what funeral home were we going to use. Mom gave her the name. The funeral home Attendant came and picked him up. Dave found out my dad had died. When we went to make arrangements, Dave showed up for that. I didn't know why he was there to help pick out the casket and make out the program. We were divorced. Dave wasn't there when I needed him, so why now?

On the day of my dad's services, we came in the family car. It was sprinkling rain. Dave came to the car with his umbrella open. He opens the door for me. Dave wanted me to walk under the umbrella with him I pulled back. I just couldn't forgive him at that time. The mortuary staff helped me out of the Limousine with an umbrella so I wouldn't get wet. Mrs. Reed, Dave's mom was at my dad's service. Dave sat up front with the family. Dave and the children cried so much. I had to be strong for my mom and siblings. My dad's service was packed. I didn't know he was liked by so many people. People were standing outside. Standing room only. I was angry because Dave was not there for me or my family. When Dave was needed the most, he was running up and down the roads with women. My dad had to go back and forth to the doctor. The air conditioner had gone out in their car. I gave Mom and Dad my car to use because I didn't want them to get overheated. I was working nights at that time. We knew he couldn't live, but when it happened it felt like someone was ripping my gut out. I was so distorted. It took me a while before I could go to the cemetery to put flowers. My brother Mel went to the grave site and he would cry at the grave site every time he visited.

My son Ron and his spouse had twins that November, a boy and a girl. They were so tiny they stayed in the hospital for a month and a half. The boy was the oldest. I was so proud of my grand babies and Dave loved those babies too. He spent a lot of time with them.

He took me back to court again, but I didn't go. He wanted to split holidays for the children to stay with him. I told them I had a class, and I couldn't attend but the children were old enough to decide what they wanted to do. They were okay with that. When Thanksgiving came, our daughter, Crystal, went to stay with him. He was staying with a woman named Camille. He had an off-and-on relationship with Camille. Camille left and went out of state to visit with her children and ex-husband. He left Crystal with Camille's mother and was with another woman. My child was robbed of her time with me and her brothers.

My brother Mel stepped in and helped where needed. He had an extra car he let my son Drew have. Drew was working and in school. I worked Monday through Friday days. On Friday evening, that was time for me, Drew, and Crystal to eat out. On Saturday, I would go out with a friend and Sunday was church for me and my family. Drew thought he was the man of the house so when I went somewhere on Saturday, he gave me a curfew and was on the sofa until I got home. Boys would be afraid to call my house for Crystal because Drew would tell them to stop calling his sister Crystal. Crystal would get upset because she was sixteen and her brother was running all the boys off.

A lot of people who I met after the divorce told me they never knew Dave had a wife he stayed in the clubs. I found out more after the divorce than I did before the divorce.

My sister Lynn's friend Percy told her Dave would meet his lady friends in the bar or he would walk in there all hugged up with a woman. I guess that was when he was supposed to be working his second job.

Jack and Debra seemed to be doing well. Debra was in nursing school and working weekends. Jack did all the cooking and cleaning. This was a younger woman so I guess he was trying to impress. Finally, Debra finished school. Debra worked in the hospital for a year and then took assignments with travel nursing. Debra was contracted out for six weeks at a time. They didn't have any children. Debra had been married before. Jack and Debra were buying a house together. When Debra came back from an assignment, she asked him for a divorce. Debra told Jack she would pay half of the mortgage. She moved to Kenner. Debra's niece was getting married. Debra asked Jack not to come to the wedding, but Jack ignored her and went to the wedding anyway. When Debra arrived at the wedding and saw Jack, she confronted him. Debra said Jack didn't I ask you not to come? So, Debra got back in her car and headed back to Kenner. Debra didn't keep her word about paying half of the mortgage. Jack lost the house. Jack moved into an apartment. I guess what goes around comes around.

When I was married to Dave, I was always embarrassed when I saw people because I felt like everybody knew what was going on in my marriage. I always kept my head down. Once I got the divorce, I held my head up and chest out. I felt like a burden had been lifted off my shoulders.

After the divorce, Dave told Crystal how many sisters and brothers she had. Before the divorce, he would always say he only had three children; Ron, Drew, and Crystal. Dave told

Crystal he had one daughter in California he had never met. I thought he had met her. I had heard about a baby when we were engaged. That's why I had mailed him his engagement ring back.

Lots of guys were calling me on my job or home phone since I was available. Most were married and I had to tell them what bridge to jump off. I don't want to share. I must be first, not second. I don't want to hear that you were home with your wife for the holidays or you will see me later. When it's cold out there I want somebody to hold me. Sneaking around that's not my style.

I went out on a couple of dates, but soon gave up. It seemed like nobody wanted to commit or somebody young was looking for you to take care of them. The first thing they asked you was "What kind of work do you do?" I ignored that question and asked, "What kind of work do you do?" I would get answers like custodian, and telecommunications.

For the young guys, I would say "You're too young," and they would say, "Age doesn't matter." I didn't reply I just thought they wanted me to buy them some tennis shoes.

I prayed for God to send me a good husband. I was tired of looking. So, one day my phone rang. It was my cousin Nick calling from his job. He was an electrician working at one of the plants. He had a guy next to him named Lee who was single and interested in meeting me. Nick put him on the phone. We talked I asked him to describe himself. He said 5'11" 220 pounds, with black hair with some gray mixed and brown eyes. I described myself as 5' 6" fair skin, 155 pounds, brown hair, hazel eyes. He wanted to meet for lunch. I told him what I was driving; a white Mazda 626, and he told me he would be driving a brown Chevrolet Silverado truck. We met at a restaurant. The food was good. I enjoyed the conversation, but he was a little on the heavy side.

I just knew God had answered my prayer. I had asked God for a secure man, a Christian man, a good provider, and financially stable. Not a man who loved to drink alcohol or smoke.

He visited my house. He asked me to come to his house and I did. He had three large dogs so I was afraid to get out of the car. He had to get me out of the car. Once I got into the house, he showed me the birds, two parrots and one cockatoo. The birds looked at me from head to toe. I don't think they liked me.

Lee had steaks marinating for me and him. I saw two more steaks marinating in the refrigerator so, I assumed he had another date the next day or later that night.

Whenever Lee and I talked, he always had money issues. Lee had two children to whom he had to pay child support. The child support was taken from the top so when he got his check it was taken out. Christmas was coming soon and he asked me what I wanted. Of course, I am not hard to please so I said it was up to him. Three days before Christmas, he told me he couldn't get me a present, he said: "I am going to get you a gift later". I had gotten him a gift, but I returned it to the store. I told Lee "Whenever you're ready we can exchange gifts".

Lee had taken me with him one day to the feed store. He had an account set up so he could feed the dogs and birds. He didn't know the difference between male and female birds so, Lee had to have them X-rayed. Lee found out he had all females. To me, feed and X-rays cost money. Why didn't Lee give up some of that or get a second job?

His pets became his family when his wife and children left him.

He called again to talk about his problems, and I told him I had enough of my own problems. I told Lee I was going on vacation to get my groove back.

Six months later, Lee called and said "I have your Christmas present; two gift cards and some mustard greens". The plant where he worked gave them gift cards. I guess he forgot he had told me that. I hope somebody enjoyed the gift cards and the mustard greens because I never went and got the gifts. That was how that relationship went. Sometimes we think it's God's works, but that was the works of the devil. He was seeing me and other women too. I had been through that before and didn't want to deal with a relationship like that anymore. That was the last time I heard from him.

I couldn't put my heart out there yet; going out was all I wanted.

No commitment. I had been hurt too many times. All I was interested in was, going out to dinner and dancing. I had to finish raising my children.

I was very angry after the divorce. I was thinking about how Dave had treated me; all the extra marriage affairs. The times he made excuses like that he was going to other places like Mason meeting, but was off somewhere with another woman. He would get another man to say they were going to a function. Dave would use all kinds of excuses anything, that was convenient for him. What hurt was, Dave using my family as well as me. I felt it was okay to use me, but my family is off-limits. That was plain crude. You must answer to God when you mistreat people. I guess Dave thought he was above that.

Lots of Christmases went by and I didn't have anybody, but I had my children. I always cooked a lot. One Christmas Ron the barber, had an older guy friend, around my age and he introduced me to him. He wasn't my type, seems like he liked bourbon. I know I couldn't compete with bourbon and wasn't about to try. We all went to the bowling alley. We had a good time. It was so funny when Crystal's friend Keith, got ready to roll his ball he went sliding down the lane with the ball. A good laugh is healthy that was just what I needed. Drew and his friend Ann, Ron, and his spouse Angel all got a good laugh.

On my birthday or Mother's Day, I would get a call from Dave. I didn't understand because we were divorced. Why is Dave calling? I thank Dave for the call. I never buy into the calls. Maybe he was calling because we had children together.

My aunt Mae wanted her house washed and painted; she asked me how to get in contact with Dave, so I gave her Dave's number. Aunt Mae got in touch with Dave. He went to her house and gave her an estimate. The estimate was reasonable for her so she let him have the job. Dave started the paint job. Dave was bragging about Camille's dad being so young. Dave also said he may be gray on top, but wasn't gray down below. My Aunt Mae is in her seventies and was told that. Dave needs help.

Dave was living with Camille and had proposed to another woman. Dave was always cheating on Camille. Dave had left Camille and brought another woman to California. Camille started calling Dave while he was out there in California. Dave left Mattie, the woman he brought out there with him. Mattie had helped him drive out there. Mattie had to call her family and ask them to send her money to come home. I guess Mattie found out

Dave was talking to Camille while they were out there together. Dave drove back without help. I guess he didn't need any help in the beginning.

Dave made it back to Camille's house. Camille was thinking he was out there visiting his sister.

A few months after going back to Camille, Dave proposed to a woman named Barbara. He had borrowed money from Barbara. When they went out to eat Barbara always paid for the meals. Barbara called the house to speak to the children about being in the wedding. The children agreed to be at the wedding. Barbara told them what colors they needed to wear and the wedding date which was going to take place on Easter Sunday after the service. The closer it got to Easter, Dave started coming around less. I don't know if Barbara knew Dave was living with Camille. My oldest son Ron would start laughing every time we started talking about the wedding. Ron would say Daddy is not going to marry Barbara she is not his type. When it was even closer to Easter, Dave stopped coming around. The wedding didn't happen, as Ron said.

Barbara was angry, so she called my daughter. Barbara told Crystal to tell her dad, Dave, that she wanted her money back. I guess Dave wasn't taking Barbara's calls. Crystal didn't have anything to do with that money deal. That was between Dave and

Barbara. Barbara called several more times asking Crystal to tell Dave she wanted her money. Barbara finally stopped calling. Barbara probably never got her money.

The relationship with Mattie, who went to California with Dave ended, since he left her out there in California, and her family had to send her money to come home. Dave left her for Camille. Dave opened a savings account for Camille when they got back together.

A friend of mine named Deloris gave me her friend's telephone number. She had met him in some classes she had taken. She was back in school taking classes to be a nurse practitioner. Deloris was divorced herself, no children. Deloris was still looking for Mr. Right herself. I called her friend Steve and we talked. If I didn't call him, Steve would call me. We made plans to meet after school for dinner. Steve was working in another town that was 30 minutes from where I lived. We met on a Tuesday evening around 6:00 p.m. at Jeff's Seafood. WOW, when I saw him; he was so good-looking and handsome. We went into the restaurant; no wait time we were seated. We looked over the menu and placed our order. The waiter was named Jane. Jane served our food. She came back to check if everything was okay. Jane was asking, "Do we need anything else" with her eyes on Steve. Jane didn't care if I was satisfied or not. Jane was trying to hit on Steve. I know having a guy that look that good meant I was going to have problems with other women. Steve's good looks can get him any woman he wants, why is it taking him so long? Steve was married and had a son. Steve's wife was killed in an automobile accident. Steve's son is a teenager. Steve keeps himself busy. Steve worked on his off days in retail. I just considered him a friend, nothing more. We would talk on the phone.

My daughter would attend church with my mom. A few men in the church would tell my daughter to tell me hello. When she went to school, a teacher would tell her all the time to tell me she said hello. Finally, one day I called that teacher. He was single. His wife had left him with two children to raise. We started talking and going out to dinner. The children at school said he kept a smile on his face now that we were going out. They were tired of seeing him looking sad day in and day out.

I had gone to high school with him; I had seen him around, but I was never interested. I always had to have a guy who played basketball or football—someone you might say was popular. This guy was a bookworm. Surprisingly we had a lot in common. Will I be able to trust a man?

Freddie's sister Ollie, was a beautician and my mom and I would go to her shop. Ollie came from a large family. When I went to Ollie's shop, which was next door to her house, we never saw her sisters or brothers. I always wondered where they were. Their house was very clean not a dish in the sink. Then I found out they were all out in the field. Their dad raised a large garden and sold vegetables. They would go into the field early in the morning before school and then get ready for school. When they got home from school, they had to work in the field again. when they finished in the field they would clean up, eat, do homework, sleep, and start the cycle all over again. Most of them went to college, the military, or trade school or started their own business.

Freddie was everything I prayed for financially stable, secure, and religious. He was not a smoker, he was a man that didn't go to clubs. He taught school and tutored on Tuesdays and Thursdays to help the children pass the leap test. On Friday and Saturday nights, he would work as a security guard. On Sundays, he would still go to church after getting off that morning from a twelve-hour night shift. After church, he would sleep, then get up and make lesson plans for the next week. He kept busy. I guess he just couldn't help it; he was brought up that way.

When I started going out with Freddie my dryer broke. Freddie told me he didn't want me to go to the laundromat. Freddie brought me to the store to pick out a dryer to be delivered to me. I had a bad experience at the laundromat before. This young guy in his thirties drives a white Toyota truck and would always pull up to laundromats; gets out of his truck goes into the laundromat with one pair of ladies' panties goes to the sink where you can hand wash or soak a garment. He wets the panties and then put the panties in the dryer. In the next step, he starts a conversation with the ladies. He always has on a pair of shorts that's so short that when he crosses his legs his scrotum sack is showing. Step three when the lady's panties dry he puts them on. All the ladies start running out of the laundromat. He was reported to the owners and the police were notified. He seems to start hanging out at another laundromat.

My car needed CV joints. Freddie put my car in the shop and had that done. I had lawn service every other week and my grass is cut. Freddie told me to cancel the service he was going to mow the lawn. This had to be "Mr. Right". Freddie had stepped up to the plate.

Freddie and I had been together for two years. Freddie made reservations at the Top of the Tour restaurant. We looked at the menu the waitress gave us. I ordered crawfish seven ways. Freddie ordered the seafood platter. The food was good. After eating Freddie pulled out a box and when he opened the box Freddie asked Lisa will you marry me? I was just stunned, excited, and tearing up. I said yes. It had been nine years since my divorce. I was glad Freddie had proposed after dinner, if he had proposed to me before dinner, I wouldn't have been able to eat, I would have been too full to eat.

The waitress put the bill on the table.

After we got engaged; I found out Freddie always had a crush on me in high school. I never knew that. Students who went to school with us said they were so glad for me and Freddie to be getting together. I guess what's meant to be will be.

We started planning our wedding. Nothing big, his best friend, Minister Harris married us. Minister Harris was excited. He was a new Minister and we were the first couple that he was performing a wedding ceremony.

We had a large reception with the band included. Freddie's family was so, excited he was getting married. they gave us a reception. Freddie's family just wanted him to be happy. Freddie and I were happy.

I saw Dave about two years later after I was married to Freddie. His health was failing and he asked me to forgive him. He wanted to apologize for the way he had treated me when we were married. He said he had talked to his minister about it. Being a Christian I said I forgive you. I guess Dave had to clear his conscience. I had cried so many times when I was married to Dave. I prayed and asked God to wipe the tears from my eyes. Dave wasn't physically abusive, but verbally abusive when he started seeing another woman. Be careful what you pray for. I want to cry sometimes for happiness or the death of a loved one, but can't.

Made in the USA
Columbia, SC
21 November 2024

47277910R00054